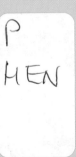

First published 1999 by Walker Books Ltd
87 Vauxhall Walk, London SE11 5HJ

2 4 6 8 10 9 7 5 3 1

Series concept and design by Louise Jackson

Words by Paul Harrison and Louise Jackson

Wildlife consultant: Martin Jenkins

Text © 1999 Walker Books Ltd
Illustrations © 1999 Sue Hendra

This book has been typeset in Lemonade.

Printed in Singapore

British Library Cataloguing in Publication Data
A catalogue record for this book is available
from the British Library.

ISBN 0-7445-6236-8

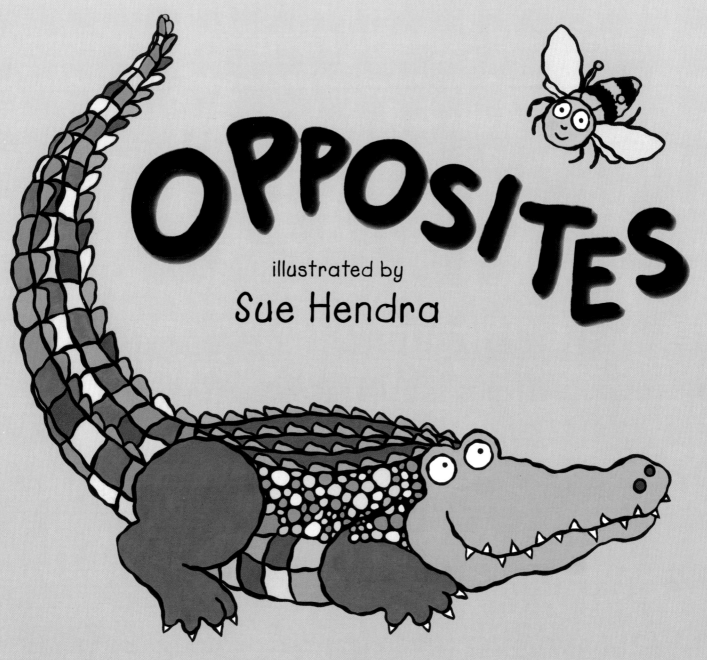

OPPOSITES

illustrated by

Sue Hendra

WALKER BOOKS

AND SUBSIDIARIES

LONDON · BOSTON · SYDNEY

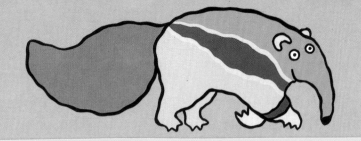

long

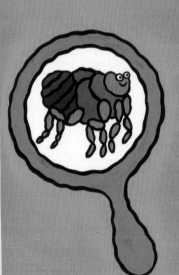

small

tall

fast

sleepy

busy

What's the opposite of fat?

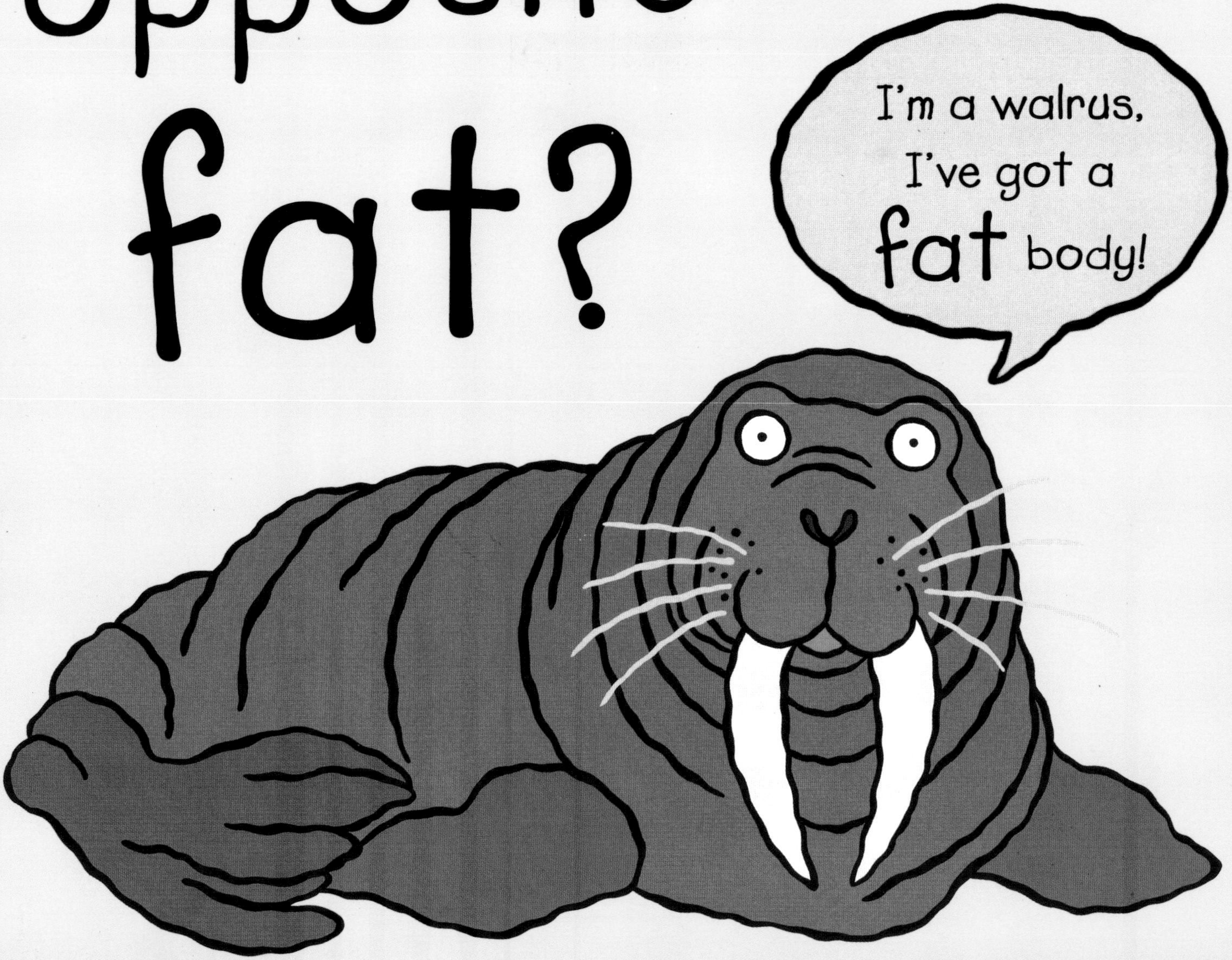

large

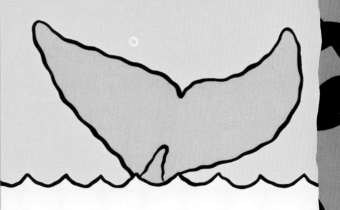

little

thin

prickly

smooth

furry

green

white

red

quiet

noisy

angry

What's the opposite of soft?

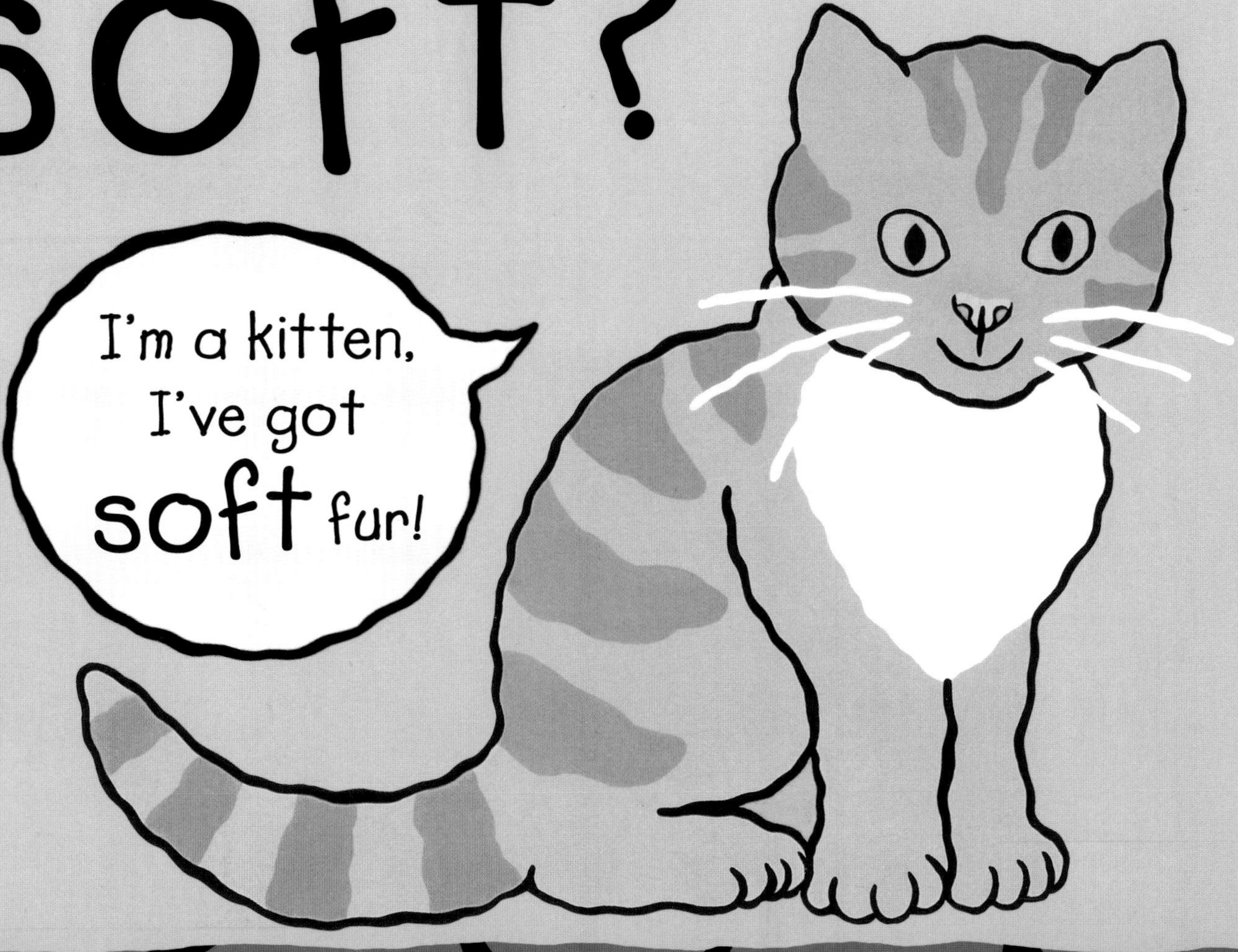

slimy

fluffy

hard

Can you match up the animal opposites?

big

slow

black

fat

loud

soft

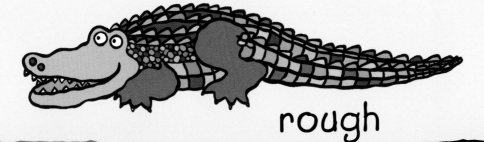
rough

smooth

white

small

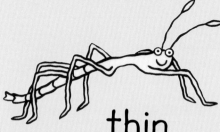

thin

fast

quiet

hard

Can you think
of any other
opposites?